Just as your hands touch this book, you set foot into
the world of poems, written by Zeina.

Zeina Qasem
Sunset Dreams

Copyright © Zeina Qasem 2022

The right of **Zeina Qasem** to be identified as author of this work has been asserted by the author in accordance with Federal Law No. (7) of UAE, Year 2002, Concerning Copyrights and Neighboring Rights.

All rights reserved. No part of this publication may be reproduced, stored in a retrieval system, or transmitted in any form or by any means, electronic, mechanical, photocopying, recording, or otherwise, without the prior permission of the publishers.

Any person who commits any unauthorised act in relation to this publication may be liable to legal prosecution and civil claims for damages.

ISBN – 9789948042587 (Paperback)
ISBN – 9789948042594 (E-Book)

Application Number: MC-10-01-8990928
Age Classification: 6-9

The age group that matches the content of the books has been classified according to the age classification system issued by the National Media Council.

Printer Name: iPrint Global Ltd
Printer Address: Witchford, England

First Published 2022
AUSTIN MACAULEY PUBLISHERS FZE
Sharjah Publishing City
P.O. Box [519201]
Sharjah, UAE
www.austinmacauley.ae
+971 655 95 202

To the ardent eyes reading this book.

Fasten your seatbelt...it's going to be a mild ride!

My deepest appreciation goes to my parents who guided me
through this action-packed journey.

Special thanks to my late grandpa; the inspiration that will never
read the book.

Who I Am

I'm the most beautiful combination

of every good that can be

        I stand up to my expectation

          What can I do, that's me

I'm a tall fruitful tree

I give away my huckleberry

        I'm a furious bird that's free

        I fly up high and never worry.

I'm the summit of the highest mountain
and the width of a river too
I'm the length of the lowest valley
and in the sky, I'm the colour blue.

I'm the bond of a mother and son
I'm the clash of wrong and right
With the long-lasting feud, I'm one
of the contenders black and white.

I'm the star shining through the night
I'm the fix of every bungle
In the dark, the shimmering light
I'm the lion, king of the jungle.

I'm the little bit of hope
when the world turns upside down
Whatever happens, won't give up
won't turn my smile into a frown.

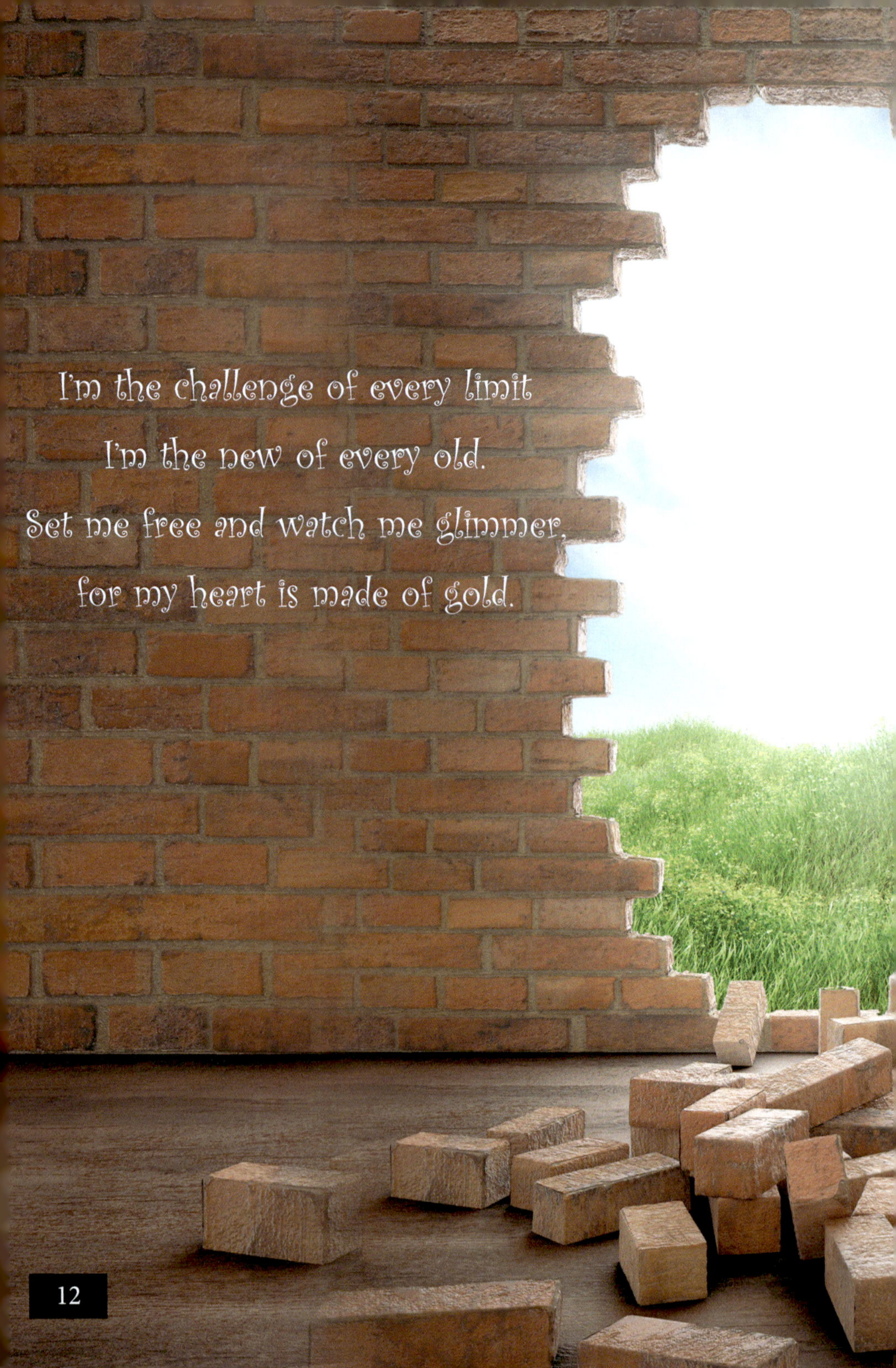

I'm the challenge of every limit
I'm the new of every old.
Set me free and watch me glimmer,
for my heart is made of gold.

I'm the flower of the farthest tree
the start and end of life
I always have faith and believe in me
I'm the blade of the sharpest knife.

I'm the beginning of every end
I'm the candle's light, I do pretend
Have I said that I'm the rhythm
The key of the unopen door

the clouds high in the sky
I fully live my entire life
of my favourite book to read
the fruit after every seed.

I'm the strength of the strongest man, the point
and core of power
The hinge which unlocks a door, the petal of a
yellow sunflower
I'm the honey in phoney people, I'm the
sweetness in your jam
I'm the moral of a fable, that's just who I am.

Tolerance

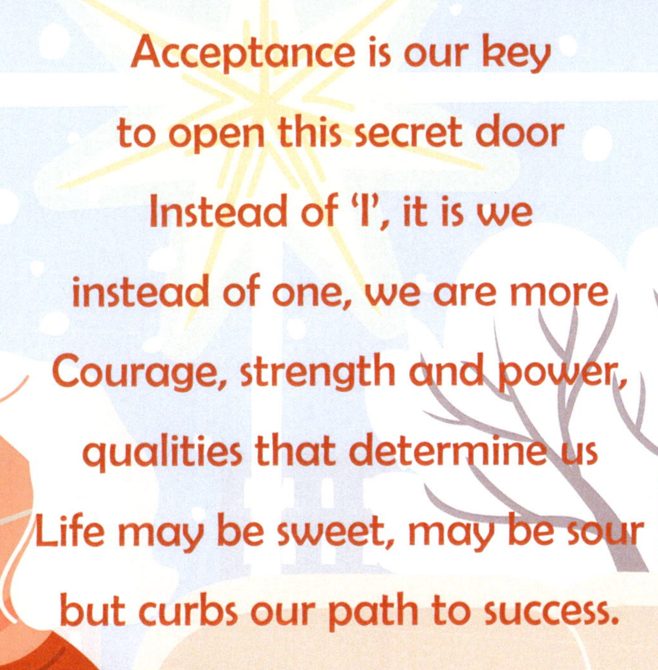

Acceptance is our key
to open this secret door
Instead of 'I', it is we
instead of one, we are more
Courage, strength and power,
qualities that determine us
Life may be sweet, may be sour
but curbs our path to success.

We are billions of beautiful hearts

side by side like shining stars.

Conquer your fears and all that hurts,

what's a hero with no scars.

What's a world with no uniqueness,
all alike and all the same
Our power is our difference,
gives lustre to the flame.

Acceptance is patience on others

Even when they make mistakes

It's sharing and giving offers

It's giving mortals a break

If peace is the destination

Then endurance is the path

Gratitude can solve the equation

Since diversity is much like math.

Empires are built by legends
not by colour of skin or hair
It's very easy to make friends
the challenge is to prove you care
So let's break through all divisions

to reach our faraway souls

We're here to unite our visions

and accomplish our many goals

Boundaries are made to be broken

like rules that make no sense

Be a voice, not an echo; be spoken

and water the seeds of tolerance.

Reading

Open your story book
and travel from page to page
Across the legends and myths
of the early stone age

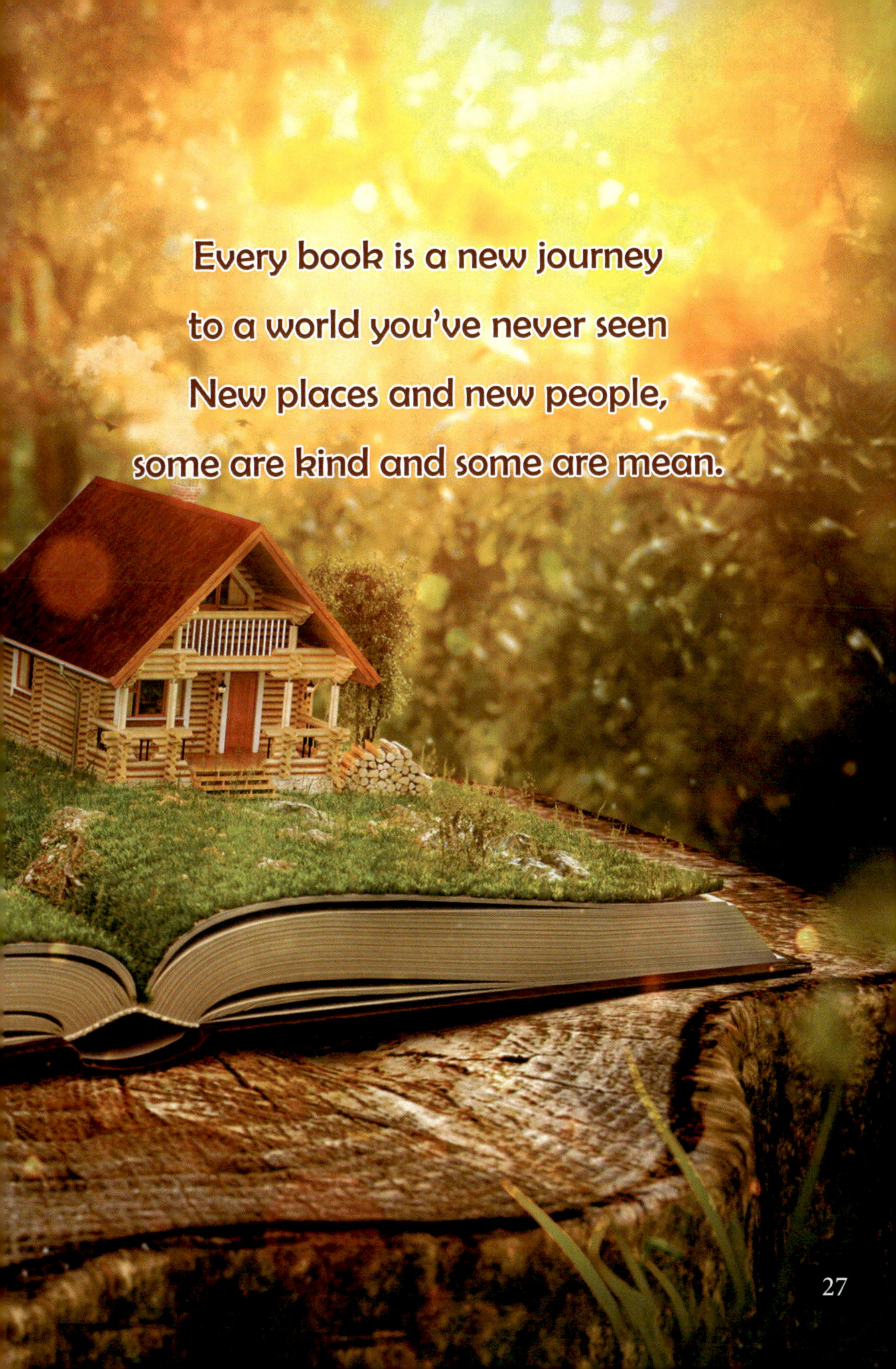

Every book is a new journey

to a world you've never seen

New places and new people,

some are kind and some are mean.

You pilot a huge ship
and sail across the seas
You get into someone's shoes
and experience what he sees

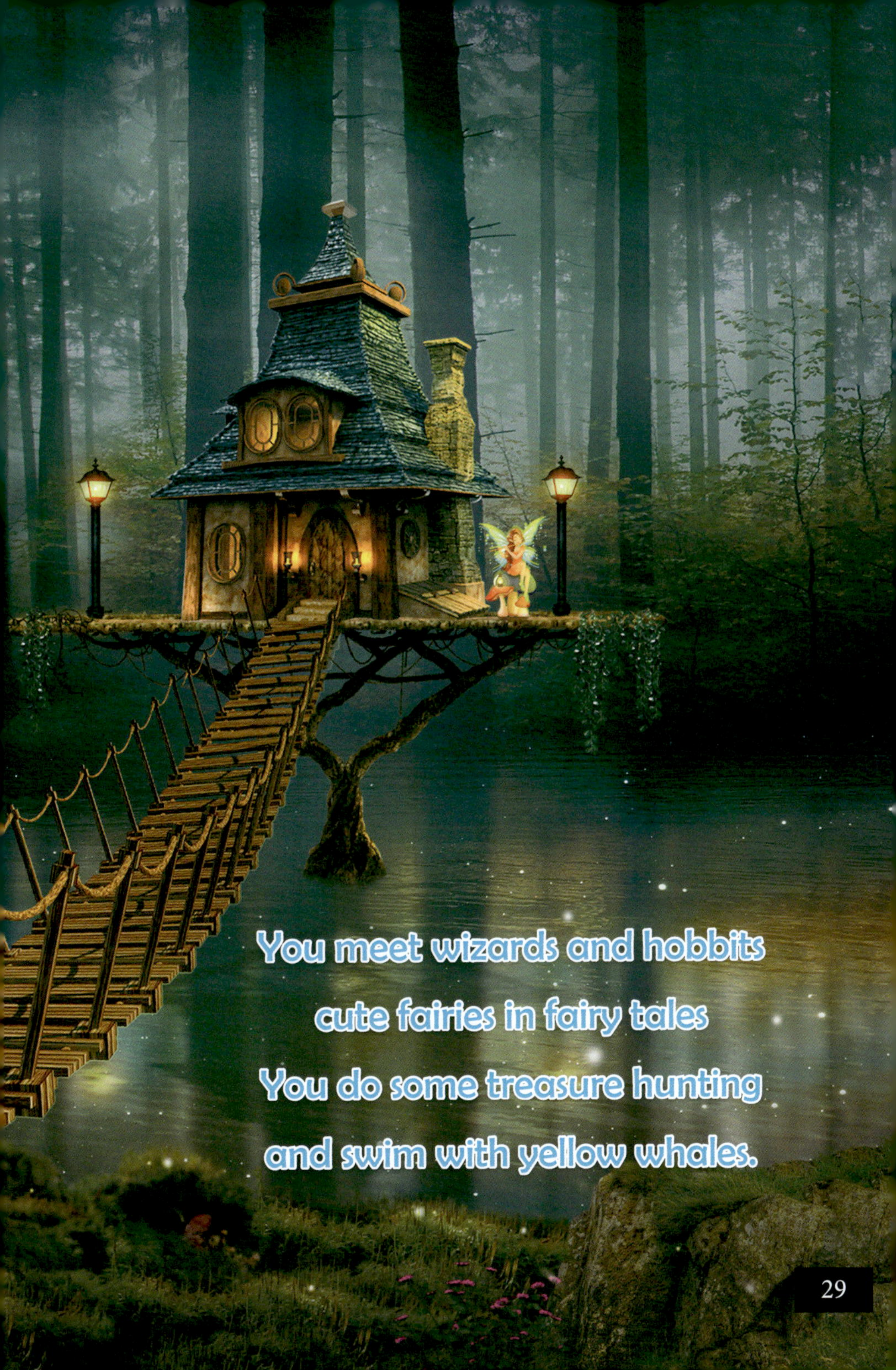

You meet wizards and hobbits
cute fairies in fairy tales
You do some treasure hunting
and swim with yellow whales.

Tales of castles and kings
and their fights over the throne.
Restless knights, magical rings
and making yourself a clone

Time travel through a black hole
and live a day with the Flintstones
Eat porridge from Goldilocks's bowl
and investigate with Sherlock Holmes.

While you're there, go to a garden

and smell nature's love

Feel the beauty of the Earth

and ride upon a dove

Take a trip to the Sun

and don't forget your spoon

To get a taste of what it's like

and at night, visit the moon.

Raiders and pirates are gloomy and vanquish all

Aircrafts and spaceships and a graceful waterfall

Dinosaurs and dragons, ones that fly and ones that don

Animals and aliens and bigfoot that can chant
Live fully the adventure and walk the lines through
Now, close this open book, for Mom is calling you.

Teachers

A very special place in my heart is taken by my one to be

That held me up from the start the one that set me free

The reign of the greatest king the words of a poet, too

Begin from you my teacher and the wisdom you get with yo

Every day is a new experience that you take us to in school

With your knowledge we shall grow for the alert was once a fool

To the last of my school days

I shall speak to every creature

of how great someone can be

Thank you, my dear teacher!

You showed us who we can become

when no one gave us hope

When our days threw us down

you lent us your rope

You are our number one

you're the wisdom and the grace

Thank you for the things you've done

to make our world a better place.

Mother

Mother knows best?
Is it true what they said?

A human made of wonder
a fantasy, I can say.
Her smile made of sunshine
her eyes, a thousand rays
Sweetness all upon her
she never grows old

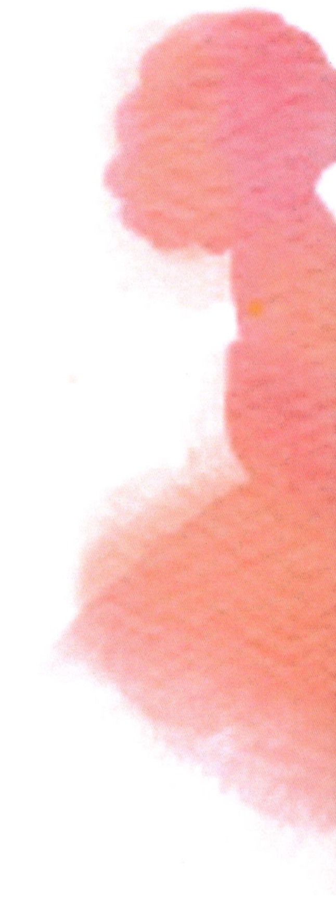

For her mind is made of love

and her heart of pure gold

She understands me when I don't

and when sad, gives me a lift

She is my ultimate superhero

she's definitely God's gift.

She is my first place to live

my only warm cuddle

The safety I want to have

as a child, she's my example

When I'm a teen, she's the shoulder

I walk with and my mind

that guides me, and when adult,

she's the best friend I can find

Your name gives me rest

your smile, a comfortable bed

"Mother knows best..."

so true what they always said.

Keyla The Koala

Mama, Mama, teach me all

help me learn the big and small

I want to grow to be so brave

give me the guidance that I crave

Mama, Mama, let's start from core

teach me rhymes, verbs and more

You're my leader, you're my sun

you're the way through which I run.

Papa, Papa, carry me through
The ups and downs along with you.

Take me through the high and low
with my knowledge I shall glow
Mama, Papa, guide me through
the right and wrong and all that's new.

Best of Who You Are

Never give up on your dream,
it has no expiration date.

Have some pride and self-esteem,
just be you and just be great.

Let the dignity crawl up your spine
Stay true lest you make a mistake.

It's always your time to shine,
just believe in the chances you take.

Life is mysterious and full of magic
only believers will succeed
Find your path and use some logic
you will seek the treasure indeed
You are who you're meant to be
no matter what anyone says
Don't wait for your turn, it's always time
to find the real path to your maze.

Decide to live this world all free
enjoy it and have an awesome life
Be the flower of the tree
and be the blade of the knife.
Stand strong and have the gut
to be truly the night's star

Don't give up no matter what
and bring the best of who you are.

Count Me In

Thank you for all the memories
we wrote together one by one

For all the happy moments we had
and all the times we had fun

Thank you for all the support
you've given to me all through

In our ups and in our downs
in our darkest days, too.

Thank you, my dear friend

for being my second half

Your warm eyes, your smile

I cherish your joyous laugh.

You are my everything
you are my intimate twin
You know when you need me
you can always count me in!

Invincible

Looking through the window
watching the world go by
I walk with the universe on me.

It's the wings with which I fly
forget all your sadness
forget all your pain.

The sun will solidly shine
after the storm and rain.

Strong people fall, but

they get back up again

No matter how hard life gets

it's up to you to reveal your reign

Let your goal be your purpose

trust yourself and you will win

Greatness comes from greater work,

better minds and better men.

I have my lifelong dream
and you surely have yours
With a dose of self-esteem
we can break through all doors.

In the air, be a tornado
in the lake, a prospering dove
Love all what you do
and do what you truly love.

Me and You

It's very hard to forget

all the times we spent

The first time we met

it feels nice to have a friend

It's very hard to forget

the times we danced and sang

moments never to regret

and all days we would hang.

A loyal friend is what you need

to have a cheerful, jolly life

Someone you care about indeed

and with whom you can thrive

It's really great to know

that you're part of a team

Has your back and never let's go,

isn't that everyone's dream?

To find someone you can trust
in happiness and in sorrow
To feel serenity and peace
to have a reason to rise in the morrow
And when you are upset
lightens your day and hugs you tight.

With all that being said
friends make your world bright
So dear friends, always know
that we will walk our lives through.

Together in the ups and downs
together, just me and you.

Literacy Day Song

Hey everyone
Come listen up
A random tempo
Is about to drop.

Men and women
Young and old
Share a vision
That shall be told.

Study and learn
Those are pillars of life
You'll have no concern
Be sure you'll thrive.

"September 8,"
UNESCO declared
That on this date
Knowledge shall be shared.

Let's sing right now
Forget your fear
Let's shout out loud
So all can hear

Challenge yourself, be bold
Because life isn't everlasting
Take risks and unfold
Life is worth the blasting.

It feels good to try
Knowledge is worth the chase
If you can't walk, just fly
past every disgrace.

Today's the celebration
So everyone will play
with words and letters
On "Literacy Day".